Product Management Secrets

Techniques For Product Managers To Boost Product Sales And Increase Customer Satisfaction

"Practical, proven techniques that will help you to make your product management job a success"

Dr. Jim Anderson

Published by:
Blue Elephant Consulting
Tampa, Florida

Copyright © 2013 by Dr. Jim Anderson

All rights reserved. No part of this book may be reproduced of transmitted in any form or by any means, electronic or mechanical, including photocopying, recording or by any information storage and retrieval system without written permission of the publisher, except for inclusion of brief quotations in a review.

Printed in the United States of America

Library of Congress Control Number: 2013923024

ISBN-13: 978-1494495916
ISBN-10: 1494495910

Warning – Disclaimer

The purpose of this book is to educate and entertain. This book does not promise or guarantee that anyone following the ideas, tips, suggestions, techniques or strategies will be successful. The author, publisher and distributor(s) shall have neither liability nor responsibility to anyone with respect to any loss or damage caused, or alleged to be caused, directly or indirectly by the information contained in this book.

Recent Books By The Author

Product Management

- Customer Lessons For Product Managers: Techniques For Product Managers To Better Understand What Their Customers Really Want

- Product Failure Lessons For Product Managers: Examples Of Products That Have Failed For Product Managers To Learn From

Public Speaking

- How To Rehearse In Order To Give The Perfect Speech: How to effectively rehearse your next speech to that your message be remembered forever!

- Secrets To Creating The Perfect Speech: How to create a speech that will make your message be remembered forever!

CIO Skills

- How CIOs Can Make Innovation Happen: Tips And Techniques For CIOs To Use In Order To Make Innovation Happen In Their IT Department

- CIO Communication Skills Secrets: Tips And Techniques For CIOs To Use In Order To Become Better Communicators

IT Manager Skills

- Secrets Of Effective Leadership For IT Managers: Tips And Techniques That IT Managers Can Use In Order To Develop Leadership Skills

- IT Manager Career Secrets: Tips And Techniques That IT Managers Can Use In Order To Have A Successful Career

Negotiating

- Learn The Skill Of Exploring In A Negotiation: How To Develop The Skill Of Exploring What Is Possible In A Negotiation In Order To Reach The Best Possible Deal

- Learn How To Argue In Your Next Negotiation: How To Develop The Skill Of Effective Arguing In A Negotiation In Order To Get The Best Possible Outcome

Miscellaneous

- Power Distribution Unit (PDU) Secrets: What Everyone Who Works In A Data Center Needs To Know!

- Making The Jump: How To Land Your Dream Job When You Get Out Of College!

Note: See a complete list of books by Dr. Jim Anderson at the back of this book.

Acknowledgements

Any book like this one is the result of years of real-world work experience. In my over 25 years of working for 7 different firms, I have met countless fantastic people and I've been mentored by some truly exceptional ones. Although I've probably forgotten some of the people who made me the person that I am today, here is my attempt to finally give them the recognition that they so truly deserve:

- Thomas P. Anderson
- Art Puett
- Bobbi Marshall
- Bob Boggs

Dr. Jim Anderson

This book is dedicated to my wife Lori. None of this would have been possible without her love and support.

Thanks for the best 21 years of my life (so far)...!

Table Of Contents

HOW DO YOU MANAGE A PRODUCT? 9

ABOUT THE AUTHOR 11

CHAPTER 1: 9 WAYS TO BECOME AN INFORMATION PRODUCT MANAGER 16

CHAPTER 2: WHAT 5 THINGS DOES A PRODUCT MANAGER NEED TO DO AT THE START OF THE YEAR? 20

CHAPTER 3: WHY PRODUCT MANAGERS NEED TO KNOW THAT COST PLUS PRICING IS WRONG, WRONG, WRONG! 23

CHAPTER 4: WHAT PRODUCT MANAGERS CAN LEARN FROM A $100,000 MISTAKE 26

CHAPTER 5: PRODUCT MANAGERS CAN LEARN FROM THE PAST: THE STORY OF THE VASA 29

CHAPTER 6: HOW PRODUCT MANAGERS PRICE PRODUCTS FOR IRRATIONAL CUSTOMERS 33

CHAPTER 7: WHAT IS A "PRODUCT VISION"? 37

CHAPTER 8: PRODUCT MANAGER TACTICS: BRINGING IN A PRICE FIGHTER 40

CHAPTER 9: WEB 2.0 PRODUCT MANAGEMENT: IT'S ALL ABOUT PARTICIPATION 43

CHAPTER 10: DRIVING LESSONS: PRODUCT MANAGERS LEARN TO RIDE THE ECONOMY 46

CHAPTER 11: HOW PRODUCT MANAGERS CAN DEAL WITH PRODUCT NAME CHANGES 49

CHAPTER 12: IN A RECESSION, PRODUCT MANAGERS KNOW CUSTOMERS WANT VALUE 52

How Do You Manage A Product?

The job of a product manager is made even more difficult by the simple fact that it really does not come with any clear instructions on how to do it correctly. As product managers we are constantly searching for ways to become better.

One of the things that every product manager quickly realizes is that their career success is very closely tied to the financial success of their product. It is the job of the product manager to make sure that his or her product is meeting the needs of their customer.

One of the most challenging aspects of creating a product that meets a customer's needs is to decide on what the right price to charge is. The goal is to charge as much as you can without exceeding what your customer's perception of the value of your product is. There are a lot of wrong ways to do this and just a few correct ways.

One of the most important things that a product manager can do is to learn from the actions of other product managers. Not all product management programs succeed. We need to teach ourselves to keep our eyes open and watch and learn from both the successes and failures of other product managers.

As though being a product manager was not hard enough, we also don't control the world in which we live. This means that we need to create plans to deal with events like product name changes, recessions, and irrational customers.

This book has been written to provide you with the insights that you are going to need in order to develop your product management skills. We'll be talking about what you need to take into consideration when you are creating a price for your product, how to start your year off on the right foot, and how to create a vision for your product.

For more information on what it takes to be a great product manager, check out my blog, The Accidental Product Manager, at:

www.TheAccidentalPM.com

Good luck!

- Dr. Jim Anderson

About The Author

I must confess that I never set out to be a product manager. When I went to school, I studied Computer Science and thought that I'd get a nice job programming and that would be that. Well, at least part of that plan worked out!

My first job was working for Boeing on their F/A-18 fighter jet program. I spent my days programming fighter jet software in assembly language and I loved it. The U.S. government decided to save some money and went looking for other countries to sell this plane to. This put me into an unfamiliar role: I started to meet with foreign military officials in order to explain what my product did.

Time moved on and so did I. I found myself working for Siemens, the big German telecommunications company. They were making phone switches and selling them to the seven U.S. phone companies. The problem was that the switches were too complicated. Customers couldn't tell the difference between one complicated phone switch from another complicated phone switch.

The Siemens sales folks were in a bind. They didn't know enough about how the switches worked to tell their customers why they should buy them. Siemens reached out into their engineering unit looking for anyone who could help the sales teams out. I put my hand up and overnight I became a product manager.

Since then I've spent over 20 years working as a product manager for both big companies and startups. This has given me an opportunity to do everything that a product manager does many, many times. I know what works as well as what doesn't work.

I now live in Tampa Florida where I spend my time managing my consulting business, Blue Elephant Consulting, teaching college courses at the University of South Florida, and traveling to work with companies like yours to share the knowledge that I have about how product managers can make their product be a success.

I'm always available to answer questions and I can be reached at:

Dr. Jim Anderson
Blue Elephant Consulting
Email: jim@BlueElephantConsulting.com
Facebook: http://goo.gl/1TVoK
Web: **www.BlueElephantConsulting.com**

"Unforgettable communication skills that will set your ideas free..."

Create Products Your Customers Want At A Price That They Are Willing To Pay!

Dr. Jim Anderson is available to provide training and coaching on the two topics that are the most important to product managers everywhere: how do I create the products that my customers want and what should I price them at?

Dr. Anderson believes that in order to both learn and remember what he says, product managers need to laugh. Each one of his speeches is full of fun and humor so that what he says "sticks" with everyone.

Dr. Anderson's Product Management Training Includes:

1. How can you segment your market?
2. What problems are your customers having right now?
3. Which of your customer's problems does your product solve?
4. How much of this problem does your product solve?
5. How much will it cost your customer if they don't fix this problem?

Dr. Jim Anderson presents over 100 speeches per year. To invite Dr. Anderson to speak at your event, contact him at:

Phone: 813-418-6970 or
Email: jim@BlueElephantConsulting.com

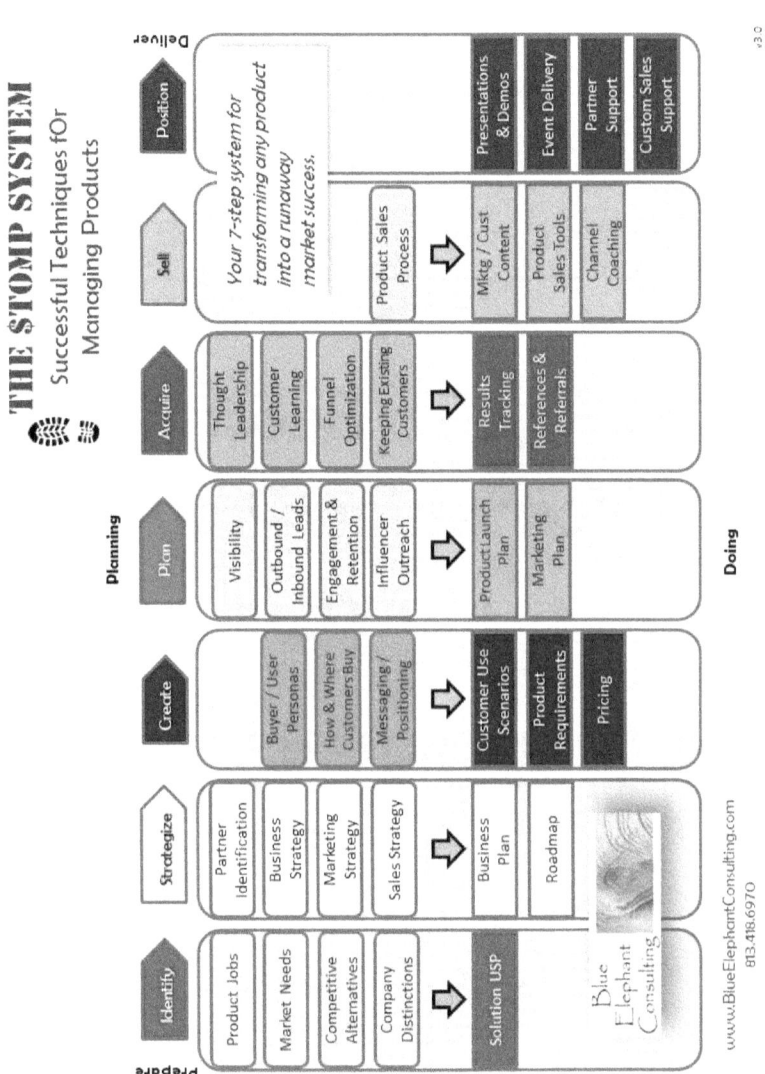

The **$TOMP™** product management system has been created by **Blue Elephant Consulting** to help product managers know what to do and when to do it in order for a product to be successful. Contact us for more information on how you can learn more.

Chapter 1

9 Ways To Become An Information Product Manager

Chapter 1: 9 Ways To Become An Information Product Manager

All too often when we think about the products or services that we are product managers for, we get hung up on the need to be able to touch something. Many of us like boxes with lights on them, CD jewel boxes that snap shut with CDs with nicely printed product labels on them, etc.

If I can touch it, then it must be a real product. Hmm, but maybe we've been missing an alternate universe of products that could boost not only our company's bottom line but also our careers...

Your company's most valuable resource is NOT its people. At least according to your accounting department. Instead the most valuable resource that your company owns is all of the data that it has collected since the day that it opened its doors.

Thomas Redman is the author of a book called **Data Driven: Profiting from Your Most Important Business Asset**. He has studied the information that companies have stored up and he's got some suggestions for us product managers.

There is a good chance that within all of this data lies a new product that you could bring to market. I'm not saying that this would be easy to do, but it would have a far better chance of succeeding than dreaming up some other risky new product.

Let's take a look at just what you would / could do to in order to turn this potential pile of gold into a product that you could successfully manage:

1. **Create New Content:** How the data that you currently have is organized and formatted may not be of any value to your potential customers. Instead, think about ways to reformat it to create new, richer or more

targeted data.

2. **Repackage, Repackage, Repackage**: Even the oldest information can take on a shiny new look if you reformat, synthesize, or filter it. Doing this can also open the door to adding data created by others to the data that you already have to create something new.

3. **Informationalize It**: Perhaps a new information product could be created by simply adding monitoring functionality to your existing products. Once you collect data about how your products are being used, perhaps this data can then be sold back to the customers who were using it!

4. **Got To Keep 'Em Separated**: Take a look at the products that you are managing right now. Are you bundling a product and data together when you sell it? Try separating the data from the product and selling it separately. Hey, it worked wonders for the Xbox!

5. **Make The Most Of Asymmetries:** Use your data to gain a better understanding of your products and your market in order to leverage any perceived differences in the value of your products or services. Things that your data tells you that nobody else knows can be key to boosting your bottom line.

6. **Sell Asymmetries**: If your data would provide insights to another firm that they can't get any other way, then consider selling it to them. Even if the data is not valuable to you, look for other firms to whom it would be valuable.

7. **Sometimes Labels Are Good**: take the time to classify your data by adding unique labels to customer types in order to help other users of your data to more easily

find what and whom they are looking for.

8. **Access Has Value:** Just by making it easier for consumers to find the data that they are looking for can create a valuable information product.

9. **Start Mining:** Often the raw data is useless. You need to mine the data and start to conduct an analysis of it. Your goal should be to gain an understanding of customer behavior and spot marketplace trends earlier than anyone else.

Chapter 2

What 5 Things Does A Product Manager Need To Do At The Start Of The Year?

Chapter 2: What 5 Things Does A Product Manager Need To Do At The Start Of The Year?

Each time we stand together at the start of another business year, it's important to realize that this time of year provides a product manager with a unique once-a-year opportunity. We can use this time of the business cycle to accomplish a few things that you just can't get done at any other time of the year.

I'm not exactly sure why this is such a special time of year, outside of the fact that we're coming out of the holidays. Considering how much of a product manager's job revolves around contacting and communicating with people, this time of year just seems to make this task that much easier.

Here's my list of what a product manager needs to do at the start of the year:

- **Plan For Success:** Forget New Year's resolutions, I'm talking about Product Manager plans. Take a few moments and picture the end of the year – what do you want to have accomplished by the end of the year?

    Keep it real – no, your product is probably not going to become the next iPhone, but if you want to still have your job it is going to have to have some level of success. This plan can be as simple as a list of 5-10 items that you jot down. Paste it on the wall and you'll be reminded of your yearly goals all year long.

- **Reconnect With Old (Business) Friends**: The madness of the end of the year is now over and everyone is in the process of trying to get their acts back together. This is a great time to reach out to everyone and connect with them in order to rekindle the relationship and get yourself in good standing for when you really need to talk to them later in the year.

- **Hoard Resources**: The neat thing about the start of the year is that nobody has a clear plan for what they want to do yet. This means that if you show up and ask for "things" – people, funding, office furniture, etc. you have a better than average chance of getting what you want. What's that phrase, "The early bird gets the worm…"

- **Visit Customers**: Just like everyone else, your customers are going to get busier as the year starts to pick up steam. If you want to have a chat with your customers about their needs and wants this can be the best time of year to have that discussion.

- **Pick Your Product's Next Features:** No matter how you go about doing it, the start of the year is THE time to plan out what features you are going to add and in what order you are going to add them.

- **Plan Your Next Product:** As product managers, we can easily become too comfortable with the products that we know and love. The truth is that all products have a life cycle and will eventually end up going away. We need to take the time to plan for what products will come next. The start of the year is a great time to do this type of activity.

Once again, the first few weeks of each year are a special time that, just like Christmas, comes only once a year. Make sure that you use this time to ensure that the rest of the year is merry for all of your products!

Chapter 3

Why Product Managers Need To Know That Cost Plus Pricing Is Wrong, Wrong, Wrong!

Chapter 3: Why Product Managers Need To Know That Cost Plus Pricing Is Wrong, Wrong, Wrong!

Come on, admit it. You like cost plus pricing. It's a product manager's best friend. We all know how this story goes, you find yourself in charge of a new product and you spend all of your time working on nailing down what features it is going to have and when it will become available. Then there is that fateful day when someone asks you "What's it going to cost?"

The simple answer is that you have no idea. If you've got competition, then you can probably use their price as a starting point. However, if you don't have clear competition, then you're sorta stuck. This is when your old friend Mr. Cost Plus pricing always seems to show up.

Just in case some readers don't quite know what cost plus pricing is, perhaps I should take a moment and define it for everyone. Cost plus pricing for a product is when you attempt to calculate all of the costs that went into creating it. You then add the appropriate level of margin on top of this cost and vola – you have your product's price.

We all love cost plus pricing so much because it has this aura of being a "financial way of creating pricing". I mean, if we are able to account for all costs and then price our product above that level then we are just about guaranteed that we will be profitable.

The problem with this is that all too often, we are wrong. The reason that we're wrong is because as the volume of products being created goes up, the costs of manufacturing goes down. If you are managing a service the same thing can be said – the more subscribers you have, the lower your cost per subscriber is.

Since your unit cost is changing with volume, your price will determine how much you sell. This will then impact volume which then impacts unit cost. Whew, it's all connected!

A great example of how not to use cost plus pricing was provided several years ago by the good engineers over at Wang Laboratories. They invented the first commercial electronic word processor in 1976. Their product was a big hit. They used cost plus pricing to come up with a price for this revolutionary product.

The problem that they ran into was that in the early 1980's personal computers become hot and they too offered word processing capabilities. As PC based word processing became more popular, Wang sales slowed.

This meant that their cost plus pricing required that they raise the price of their product even as their competition was reducing the cost of their products. Their pricing eventually drove away all of their customers.

So what's wrong with cost plus pricing? Simple – cost plus pricing will cause you to over-price your product when there is a weak market and will cause you to under-price your product when there is a strong market.

So what's the lesson to learn here? Hopefully, you now understand that cost plus pricing is a really bad idea. Instead, as a product manager what you need to do in order to ensure profitable pricing is to spend some time and decide on what your anticipated prices are going to be. Then, use this information to manage your costs. This type of value-based pricing needs to start BEFORE you make the investments required to breathe life into your product.

Chapter 4

What Product Managers Can Learn From A $100,000 Mistake

Chapter 4: What Product Managers Can Learn From A $100,000 Mistake

As product managers we are generally quite proud of our products. We do our best to work with potential customers and collect requirements. We ride herd over our developers to make sure that a good product is developed and that it rolls out smoothly. What happens if there is then a flaw in how the customer uses the product – are we at fault?

Kai Olsen from the University of Begen wrote an interesting piece that ended up in **Computer** magazine awhile back about such an incident. This story has a lot to teach us product managers.

It turns out that there was a very ordinary bank customer in Norway who used the Internet to do much of her banking. One day she wanted to transfer a large sum of money (roughly US$100,000) to her daughter. When she keyed in the daughter's account number during the transfer, she accidentally keyed in one digit too many.

This mistake resulted in the money being sent to an unknown third party who clearly thought that they had won the lottery. This third party promptly proceeded to gamble away much of the money before the police were able to step in and confiscate the remaining part.

Needless to say, this case got a lot of press in Norway. New banking regulations were requested to prevent this kind of slip up in the future. Obviously Internet banking had a lot more risk to it than most people thought.

In this case the end user was wrong – she entered too many digits. Before pressing enter, she could have corrected her error. At the same time, the system also could have caught and corrected her error. This did not happen – the team that built the system had not put such checks into the design.

The specific details around how this error occurred were as follows. The daughter's account number was 71581555022. The user entered 715815555022. The standard length of a Norwegian account number is only 11 digits so the incorrectly entered account number was truncated to 71581555502.

To make things even more amazing: the last digit in a bank account is a modulo-11 calculated number that should catch single key typing errors and cases in which two numbers have been interchanged. However, due to an unlucky coincidence the number that she typed was a valid account number.

Clearly the end user was very upset about what had happened. She took her case to the Norwegian Complaints Board for Consumers in Banking. She ended up losing her case – they said that she made the error and has to take the responsibility for it.

The user is taking the case to a higher court. She claims that since she typed in 12 digits, it was the responsibility of the system to give her an error message instead of just dropping all digits after the 11th.

As product managers we try our best to create high quality products that will serve our customers well. This case points out a clear failure of a product manager to do this job completely. What went wrong here?

How our customers interact with our product is, if not the most important pat, than at least one of the most important parts of any product. Yes, we'd all like to have a very cool iPod / iPhone like interface that everyone raves about. However, even if we can't have that, it sure seems like it is a requirement that we have an interface that operates correctly and in a manner that won't harm our customers.

Chapter 5

Product Managers Can Learn From The Past: The Story Of The Vasa

Chapter 5: Product Managers Can Learn From The Past: The Story Of The Vasa

Oh man , do I have a story for you. How many times have we been in charge of a product when "higher powers" have come along with suggestions on how to make the product better? Or perhaps they suggest features that the product just must have before it goes out the door?

These types of suggestions can kill a product no matter how carefully you have nurtured it up to this point. The impacts can range from timelines, expenses, all the way to final product price. So much for your best laid plans.

George Neville-Neil over at the **Communications of the ACM** is well aware of events like this. He tells the story of the good ship Vasa and this tale has a lot of warnings for us Product Managers.

This is a story that starts back in 1626 when the king of Sweden, King Gustavus Adolphus, ordered the building of the Vasa. It took two years to create this ship. King Adolphus was keen to have it because at the time he was trying very hard to rule the Baltic Sea.

Just to prove to you that things really don't change, you need to understand that King Adolphus was deeply involved in the design of all of the ships in his naval fleet. Can you say "too much senior management involvement"?

Back in the 1600's, warships had one deck of cannons on both the left and the right side of the ship. The commission orders for the Vasa ordered that she be created with this design.

Now at just about this time, good King Adolphus discovered that the Poles had somehow created ships with two decks of guns on them (for a total of four decks of guns). Needless to say the King developed a serious case of cannon envy.

Since he was king and could basically do anything that he wanted, King Adolphus modified the design of the Vasa to now include two decks of guns. To the king's credit, on paper the Vasa was now the most powerful ship of its day and had a great deal of firepower.

As with all great senior management plans, this one had just one little flaw. The designers of the ship realized that there was now a problem and attempted to explain that to the king. What they had discovered was that the ship's design called for it to have too little ballast in order to support two heavy gun decks. They believed that building the ship that the king had designed would result in a ship that would be unsafe to sail.

You know how this story goes – it's good to be king. The king wanted his ship and he wanted it the way that he had designed it. The building of the ship continued.

(This is my favorite part of the story that George tells) In 1628 the ship was done and ready for initial testing. One of the tests that they did was a stability test. In this test, 30 sailors were selected and asked to run back and forth from side-to-side on the ship's deck. If the ship didn't tip over and sink then it was basically good to go. During this testing of the Vasa, the ship started to tilt wildly and they ended up cancelling the test.

You would think that this was the end of the story. But it isn't.

On August 10th, 1628, the king's mighty ship the Vasa set sail for the first time. The ship got about a mile away from the dock when a good stiff breeze came along and knocked the ship sideways, she took on too much water, and then she promptly sunk.

Of course there was an investigation in order to find out what had gone wrong. Since the king, of course, could not have been the problem, the question was who was to blame. In the end, the sinking was chalked up to an "Act of God" and forgotten.

However, in the 1960's the Vasa was raised from the sea and was placed in a museum in Stockholm. If you ever get there, make sure that you drop in and see it – a shrine to all product managers who've had to deal with meddling senior management.

Chapter 6

How Product Managers Price Products For Irrational Customers

Chapter 6: How Product Managers Price Products For Irrational Customers

Who has to deal with irrational customers – isn't "irrational" just another word for "crazy"? If you've ever had to set a price for your product, then you know what I'm talking about. No matter what price you pick (or how you pick it) people are always going to be telling you that it's the wrong price. Is everyone crazy?

When we bump into problems like this that don't seem to have any answer, it's always a good idea to go talk to an expert. In this case, the expert is Dr. Dan Ariely who is an expert in behavioral economics and who works at Duke University's Fuqua School of Business.

Oh, and by the way, he wrote the book on what goes on in our heads when we go to make buying decisions: **Predictably Irrational: The Hidden Forces That Shape Our Decisions**.

All of us with a technical bent will not be pleased to hear what Ariely has to say. His main point is that when we go to price our products, we need to take into account that our customers will be using their irrational human behavior when they are deciding to buy us or not. Dang - I hope that he's got some suggestions for us...

Ariely's first tip is for those product managers who are dealing with a revolutionary new product – one that really does not have a direct competitor. Just what do you price something like this at? His suggestion? Price it so that your customer can compare it with something that they are already familiar with. Why do this?

It turns out that we human beings find that making decisions is quite tough to do. So when we encounter a new type of product, we struggle to place a value on it because we see it as existing by itself – in isolation. More often than not, what we end up doing is relying on old, past decisions (including comparisons to other products).

A great example of this is the TIVO DVR product. Just how do you go about pricing something like that when it first came out? The value is time saved, but what customer is going to sit down and calculate how much their time is worth and then figure out how much time they might save if they bought a TIVO?

We all rely on our past impressions in order to infer value on new things. This means that product managers who want to understand how our potential customers make decisions about our products will need to take the actual decision process into account. Which is why relativity is so important…

Ariely also thinks that we need to know that the relativity of prices is a critical part of the customer's decision process. If you were the TIVO product manager and you told your customers to compare the product to a VCR, then your customers are going to be unwilling to pay $500 for your product. However, if you told them to compare it to a computer, then they'll be more than willing to spend $500 to buy it. Or you can do what Apple did…

Ariely's final point is that the price that you use to define the value of your product will stick in your customer's mind for a very, very long time. The most recent case study for how this works is Apple's iPhone.

When first introduced, the iPhone was priced at $600. Almost immediately they slashed the price to $400, apologized to initial purchasers and gave them price difference refunds if they asked for them. Silly mistake on Apple's part or clever pricing?

It may have been clever pricing: now a $400 iPhone seemed like a great deal when compared to the initial $600 price. When the price dropped to $200 it now looks like a fantastic deal because we all still remember the initial $600 price.

Chapter 7

What Is A "Product Vision"?

Chapter 7: What Is A "Product Vision"?

I was working with a client the other day that had a unique problem: they needed a vision for their product. Now, I'm pretty familiar with the whole "vision" thing as it applies to a company – it's that thing that you put on the wall that nobody ever reads. However, this was the first time that I had someone ask me for one for a product.

My client had been supplying products to different firms that were operating in a market for years. However, they now saw the opportunity to start supplying bundles of their products (can you say "solutions"?) to their customers.

However, they were going to be hard pressed to explain why they were all of a sudden showing up in this market with these new solutions. What was there motivation?

Now we all know that the motivation was to make more money – all business operate this way. However, you can't really make that the basis of an advertising campaign.

Instead, my client needed a solid story that would provide a justification for what they were doing today as well as any future products they might roll out farther down the line.

I must confess that right off the bat I was stumped. I mean, a vision just for a line of products?

I did a bit of poking around and I discovered that the firm's CEO had been doing some talking at trade shows. His basic message had been that the market was broken and that it was going to take some fundamental changes in order to set things straight.

Hey – this was something that I could use! With a bit of wordsmithing, I took the CEO's words and turned them into a simple vision statement for the product line – we're introducing these products to help fix what's wrong in the marketplace.

It had the right time frame for a vision (very long) and it pointed towards a goal that everyone in the market really wanted to move towards. It turns out that this was just about perfect – a feel good vision that could be used for a very long time.

Chapter 8

Product Manager Tactics: Bringing In A Price Fighter

Chapter 8: Product Manager Tactics: Bringing In A Price Fighter

Times are tough. Your product, your baby, is struggling. New competitors are showing up in your market providing your customers with lower cost alternatives.

Try as you might, your sales teams are just not having any luck convincing your customers to shell out the extra bucks for **your Cadillac product**. What's a product manager to do?

Lots of product managers attempt to deal with low cost competitors by **cutting the price** on their product. This can be a big mistake.

Rafi Mohammed who wrote **The Art of Pricing: How to Find the Hidden Profits to Grow Your Business** says that once you start to do this, you'll end up devaluing your product. Once things get better, you may find that you can't raise your prices.

How about introducing a new product – **a price fighter**? Yes, that might seem just a bit counter intuitive right now to launch a new product, but it just might save your bacon.

A price fighter product is a low cost version of your standard product. The key is to sell this product under a different name so that your customers don't get confused.

You are already aware of lots of other firms that are currently using price fighters:

- Procter & Gamble: premium product – **Pampers**, price fighter – **Luvs**
- Delta Airlines: premium product – **Delta**, price fighter – **Song**

- Anheuser-Bush: premium product – **Budweiser**, price fighter – **Bush**

The list goes on and on (**Black & Decker** / **Dewalt**, **Sony** / **Aiwa**). Price fighter products do two things: they allow you to preserve the pricing that you use for your premium product (while still allowing the company to make enough money to stay in business), and they take revenue away from your competition.

Reed Holden wrote a book called **Pricing with Confidence: 10 Ways to Stop Leaving Money on the Table**. He pointed out that if you are planning on introducing a price fighter product, then **you need to move quickly**. Holden points out that Motorola took their time introducing cheaper cell phones and this allowed Nokia to jump in and own that part of the market.

Chapter 9

Web 2.0 Product Management: It's All About Participation

Chapter 9: Web 2.0 Product Management: It's All About Participation

As a product manager you know that you should be using shiny new **Web 2.0** stuff to market your product. However, the sticky question is what exactly should you be using and, oh by the way, just how should you be using it?

Traditional marketing has always been pretty much a one-way street – you to them. However, the beauty of all of these new fanged Web 2.0 tools is that they pretty much turn this all upside down: now marketing can be a **two-way conversation**. With such great opportunities also comes great challenges. That's what we need to talk about!

The most powerful thing that a product manager can do is to set up an **online community** that his/her existing and potential customers can use. The key here is to allow them to network amongst themselves and to allow them to talk about whatever they want to.

A toy company set up such a community in order to get opinions from mothers. The mothers came and then used the community to set up their own blogs and proceeded to write about family issues. This was **pure gold** for the company because they were able to learn a great deal more about their customers this way.

The key is to get your customers to come to your community and to **participate**. There are lots of ways to make this happen. Two of the most popular are **cash rewards** and **peer recognition**. The attraction of cash (or products) is obvious; you just have to make sure that everyone understands that these prizes are only available to members of the online community.

Awarding "stars" or "points" to users every time they post something or interact with the site is another way to create an online sense of community. Everyone likes to be **recognized** and this is a great way for both you and the online community to identify the **experts** amongst you.

One final thought is that a **moderator** for your online product community is critical. It's the Internet and we all know how wild things can get if they are left to their own devices. The role of a moderator is to keep conversations going, make sure that everyone feels as though their voice has been heard, police what is being posted, and to basically maintain order.

It's also the role of the moderator to make sure that the consensus of the online community gets **communicated back to the product manager**. After all, that's why you created the Web 2.0 online community in the first place!

Chapter 10

Driving Lessons: Product Managers Learn To Ride The Economy

Chapter 10: Driving Lessons: Product Managers Learn To Ride The Economy

The Dow Jones Average plunges 700 points in a day. Then it rises 500 points the next day. Your best customer just suddenly goes out of business one day (Enron, Lehman Brothers, Circuit City, etc.). Sure seems like no Product Manager could ever learn to deal with **the worst economy** in a generation...

Wrong! Our brother and sister product managers in Eastern Europe, South Africa, and Latin America have been dealing with markets like this for a long time. They see this as a time to take over rivals, implement bold ideas, and generally **boost their business**. Want to learn their secrets?

Martin Roth and Richard Ettenson over at the Wall Street Journal have been doing some digging in order to find out how product managers can **make the best of tumultuous times**.

One thing that they've discovered is that when the economy tanks, this is a great time to prepare for the future by getting your customers to **trade up**. This sounds rather backwards right?

I mean when times get tough, people tend to trade down. Even though the margins on your stripped down products are skinner, most product managers think that SOME sales are better than none.

In emerging markets, product managers have realized something much deeper. They get their customers to **trade UP to premium products** even though corporate budgets may be tight.

The key to doing this successfully is to be very, very careful about how you **set the prices for the different tiers of your**

product offerings. You can't make the price differences between basic and premium products too much or else your budget constrained customers will get turned off.

Instead, what you need to do is to accept a lower profit margin on your premium products – in fact, lower than most companies are normally willing to accept. However, we are not currently living in normal times. You want to signal to your buyers **that your premium products are a good value**.

If you can signal to your customers that your premium brand is offering them more value for the money, then they will be both **more willing** to trade up to it as well as to stick with it during hard times.

An example might make all of this a bit clearer. Say your product is a software package that you sell in a basic package for 20 users that you price at $10,000, an advanced package priced at $12,000, and a premium package priced at $13,000.

When the economy sours, what you want to do is change your pricing to what use an approach that's called line symmetry. Now all of your packages are priced the same ($10,000) but the number of user licenses changes to 20 for the basic package, 17 in the advanced, and 14 in the ultimate.

Now not only is **the overall price lower**, but the **incremental price** for each user license is smaller and more consistent.

Using this type of pricing scheme during a recession makes it easier both economically and emotionally for your customers to **trade up** to your premium products. Hard times call for novel product manager ideas.

Chapter 11

How Product Managers Can Deal With Product Name Changes

Chapter 11: How Product Managers Can Deal With Product Name Changes

Just image this scenario: you're sitting there at "mid-sized company, Inc." when one day your boss walks up to you and says "we've just been bought by really-big-company, Inc." Ok, you say to yourself, how much of a big deal to my successful product can this be?

Well one thing that you may not have thought of is that although your product name worked for your previous company, it may not fit with the branding of the new company. This means just one thing – **it's time for a product name change**.

Early on in my career I was the product manager who was responsible for a small utility that pre-formatted code to prevent too many warning error messages from showing up. I had somewhat whimsically named this product "NUKE216" for a variety of youthful and technical reasons.

This name was ok when only hardcore developers were the market for it. However, when it got bundled with other products, then it started to get more exposure and, you guessed it, **the name had to change**!

So what steps should a product manager take if it comes time to rename his /her product? Here are the most important:

1. **Buy In, Buy Early**: Since many different people in your company deal with your product, they may all feel some sense of ownership of it (although, of course, it is YOUR product). You need to make sure that they feel included in the renaming process even if only means that you keep them informed about the process as the new

name is picked.

2. **Direct Mail Is Your Friend**: In order to prevent your existing customers (and potential customers) from becoming confused, the old standby of direct mail is a great way to get your new (and old) name and logo into their hands.

3. **Press Time**: Getting word out to the industry press about your name change is critical. The key will be to tie the name change into something more newsworthy – a big win, a local community event, etc.

4. **Be A Tortoise**: Nobody ever said that you had to change everything all at once. One approach is to change it slowly, over time. Like the next time you get brochures printed, you use the new name.

5. **Go On A Name Hunt**: You would be amazed at how many places your old product name exists. When you change the name, you need to find ALL of these hiding spots and change them to the new name. Perhaps offering a reward for staff who find missed names can help to speed up the process.

6. **Ask Your Customers**: The experts say that it will take AT LEAST a year for you to fully change the name of a product. Keep checking with your customers to find out how the name change is going. They are the only ones who will be able to tell you how much farther you have to go.

Chapter 12

In A Recession, Product Managers Know Customers Want Value

Chapter 12: In A Recession, Product Managers Know Customers Want Value

A recession changes everything. Product managers who had everything set up and working just right have been surprised to discover that all of a sudden customers are **canceling orders and have stopped placing new orders**. What's a product manager to do?

Martin Roth and Richard Ettenson over at the Wall Street Journal have been doing some digging in order to find out how product managers can **make the best of tumultuous times**. They've interviewed lots of product managers who live in emerging markets and who have to deal with inflation, hyperinflation, and recessions.

What they've discovered is that product managers who work in such tough economies are constantly being forced to **rethink their business models** in order to be successful. A really good example of this is how wireless services are sold in emerging markets.

In the U.S. wireless services are generally sold by getting customers to buy fancy phones with sophisticated features and sign up for long term contracts. This approach **will no longer work** in the depths of a recession when customers no longer have enough money to spend on such things.

In emerging markets this type of approach to marketing and selling products has never worked. Instead, product managers have had to come up with ways to match their **customers' varying spending patterns**. During a recession, we can learn a lot from these product managers.

The approach that is used to sell wireless service in emerging markets is to sell the product in **much smaller, and cheaper,**

amounts. The product managers have realized that in order to be successful they need to make it easy for their customers to buy more of their product (minutes) when and where they want to.

This means that in developing countries, you can "refresh" your wireless minutes just about anywhere including at retail stores and at ATM machines.

This approach can be used for almost any product: make it easier for your customers to buy your product by selling it in smaller quantities and then making it easier for them to **get more when they need it**!

It's from the forge of failure that the steel of success is formed.

Hard Work Does Not Guarantee Success, But Success Does Not Happen Without Hard Work.

- Dr. Jim Anderson

Create Products Your Customers Want At A Price That They Are Willing To Pay!

Dr. Jim Anderson is available to provide training and coaching on the two topics that are the most important to product managers everywhere: how do I create the products that my customers want and what should I price them at?

Dr. Anderson believes that in order to both learn and remember what he says, product managers need to laugh. Each one of his speeches is full of fun and humor so that what he says "sticks" with everyone.

Dr. Anderson's Product Management Training Includes:

1. How can you segment your market?
2. What problems are your customers having right now?
3. Which of your customer's problems does your product solve?
4. How much of this problem does your product solve?
5. How much will it cost your customer if they don't fix this problem?

Dr. Jim Anderson presents over 100 speeches per year. To invite Dr. Anderson to speak at your event, contact him at:

Phone: 813-418-6970 or
Email: jim@BlueElephantConsulting.com

Blue Elephant Consulting

Speaking. Negotiating. Managing. Marketing.

Photo Credits:

Cover - By: Sarah Horrigan
http://www.flickr.com/photos/horrigans/

Chapter 1 - By: Kevin Dooley
http://www.flickr.com/photos/pagedooley/

Chapter 2 - By: Carol
http://www.flickr.com/photos/71256895@N00/

Chapter 3 - By: 401(K) 2012
http://www.flickr.com/photos/68751915@N05/

Chapter 4 - By: EP Technology
http://www.flickr.com/photos/ep_technology/

Chapter 5 - By: Carl Mueller
http://www.flickr.com/photos/carl_mueller/

Chapter 6 - By: zoetnet
http://www.flickr.com/photos/zoetnet/

Chapter 7 - By: Rev. Xanatos Satanicos Bombasticos (ClintJCL)
http://www.flickr.com/photos/clintjcl/

Chapter 8 - By: Boston Public Library
http://www.flickr.com/photos/boston_public_library/

Chapter 9 - By: James Cridland
http://www.flickr.com/photos/jamescridland/

Chapter 10 – By: Dean Thorpe
http://www.flickr.com/photos/aspexdesign/

Chapter 11 - By: milo tobin
http://www.flickr.com/photos/divine_harvester/

Chapter 12 - By: starmanseries
http://www.flickr.com/photos/69125796@N00/

Other Books By The Author

Product Management

- Product Development Lessons For Product Managers: How Product Managers Can Create Successful Products

- Customer Lessons For Product Managers: Techniques For Product Managers To Better Understand What Their Customers Really Want

- Product Failure Lessons For Product Managers: Examples Of Products That Have Failed For Product Managers To Learn From

- Communication Skills For Product Managers: The Communication Skills That Product Managers Need To Know How To Use In Order To Have A Successful Product

- How To Have A Successful Product Manager Career: The Things That You Need To Be Doing TODAY In Order To Have A Successful Product Manager Career

- Product Manager Product Success: How to keep your product on track and make it become a success

Public Speaking

- How To Give A Great Presentation: Presentation techniques that will transform a speech into a memorable event

- How To Rehearse In Order To Give The Perfect Speech: How to effectively rehearse your next speech to that your message be remembered forever!

- Secrets To Creating The Perfect Speech: How to create a speech that will make your message be remembered forever!

- Secrets To Organizing The Perfect Speech: How to organize the best speech of your life!

- Secrets To Planning The Perfect Speech: How to plan to give the best speech of your life

CIO Skills

- Critical CIO Management Skills: Decision Making Skills That Every CIO Needs To Have In Order To Be Able To Make The Right Choices

- How CIOs Can Make Innovation Happen: Tips And Techniques For CIOs To Use In Order To Make Innovation Happen In Their IT Department

- CIO Communication Skills Secrets: Tips And Techniques For CIOs To Use In Order To Become Better Communicators

- Managing Your CIO Career: Steps That CIOs Have To Take In Order To Have A Long And Successful Career

- CIO Business Skills: How CIOs can work effectively with the rest of the company!

IT Manager Skills

- Staffing Skills IT Managers Must Have: Tips And Techniques That IT Managers Can Use In Order To Correctly Staff Their Teams

- Secrets Of Effective Leadership For IT Managers: Tips And Techniques That IT Managers Can Use In Order To Develop Leadership Skills

- IT Manager Career Secrets: Tips And Techniques That IT Managers Can Use In Order To Have A Successful Career

- IT Manager Budgeting Skills: How IT Managers Can Request, Manage, Use, And Track Their Funding

Negotiating

- Learn The Skill Of Exploring In A Negotiation: How To Develop The Skill Of Exploring What Is Possible In A Negotiation In Order To Reach The Best Possible Deal

- Learn How To Argue In Your Next Negotiation: How To Develop The Skill Of Effective Arguing In A Negotiation In Order To Get The Best Possible Outcome

- How To Open Your Next Negotiation: How To Start A Negotiation In Order To Get The Best Possible Outcome

- Preparing For Your Next Negotiation: What You Need To Do BEFORE A Negotiation Starts In Order To Get The Best Possible Deal

Miscellaneous

- Power Distribution Unit (PDU) Secrets: What Everyone Who Works In A Data Center Needs To Know!

- Making The Jump: How To Land Your Dream Job When You Get Out Of College!

Techniques For Product Managers To Boost Product Sales And Increase Customer Satisfaction

> This book has been written with one goal in mind – to show you how to manage your product. No matter if it's setting the right price, creating a product vision, or dealing with name changes we'll show you how to do it correctly
>
> **Let's Make Your Product A Success!**

What You'll Find Inside:

- **9 WAYS TO TO BECOME AN INFORMATION PRODUCT MANAGER**
- **WHY PRODUCT MANAGERS NEED TO KNOW THAT COST PLUS PRICING IS WRONG, WRONG, WRONG**
- **WHAT IS A "PRODUCT VISION"?**
- **WEB 2.0 PRODUCT MANAGEMENT: IT'S ALL ABOUT PARTICIPATION**

Dr. Jim Anderson brings over 25 years of real-world product management experience to this book. He's managed products at some of the world's largest firms as well as at start-ups. He's going to show you what you need to do in order to make your career a success!

www.ingramcontent.com/pod-product-compliance
Lightning Source LLC
Chambersburg PA
CBHW071813170526
45167CB00003B/1288